Published by Creative Education
123 South Broad Street, Mankato, Minnesota 56001
Creative Education is an imprint of The Creative Company

Designed by Stephanie Blumenthal.

Photos by: Allsport Photography, Associated Press/Wide World
Photos, Globe Photos, NBA Photos, SportsChrome,
and UPI/Corbis-Bettmann.

Library of Congress Cataloging-in-Publication Data

Goodman, Michael E.
Grant Hill / by Michael E. Goodman.
p. cm. – (Ovations)
ISBN 0-88682-831-7

1. Hill, Grant–Juvenile literature. 2. Basketball players–United States–
Biography–Juvenile literature. I. Title. II. Series.
GV884.H55G66 1997   96-46220
796.323'092–dc20
[B]

5 4 3 2

OVATIONS

GRANT
HILL

BY MICHAEL E. GOODMAN

Creative Education

REFLECTIONS

The letters and questions pour in every day, by regular mail and e-mail. "Who was your favorite player growing up?" "What was it like to play in the Olympics?" "Do you want to be a coach after you retire?" Every letter receives an answer, by mail or via the Internet. He is bombarded by requests for autographs, and he routinely signs his name without charging children for the cherished signature. Unlike some other pro athletes, he welcomes the idea of being a good role model for

children, and he takes the responsibility seriously. When companies hire him to endorse their products, he makes certain that his contracts also call for funding for projects to help needy kids play basketball.

Those are just some of the reasons that everyone has a good word to say about Grant Hill. He has quickly become one of the most popular basketball players in the country because of his talent and his personality. In an era when many professional athletes come across to the public as selfish and boastful, Grant appears humble and sincere. He is also a special kind of winner because he values team accomplishments over personal achievements. As a result, Grant's teams have nearly always been successful, even as he has piled up personal honors.

And, along with everything else, he is an outstanding basketball player with tremendous skill and versatility on the court. In just his second season as a pro, for example, Grant was the only player in the league to lead his club in minutes played, scoring average, rebounding, assists, and blocked shots. He is the complete package—as a person and a player.

His own sports heroes and idols are such men as Julius Erving and Arthur Ashe, quiet superstars who made a lasting mark on their sports—and on society. He hopes to follow in their footsteps. He has adopted the motto "Change the Game" for his career and intends to bring a new style and new ideas to professional basketball.

Grant Hill is a popular guest on such talk shows as The Tonight Show with Jay Leno, previous page. The Olympic gold-medal winner understands the importance of education and physical fitness. He's always eager to share his insight and enthusiasm with young people.

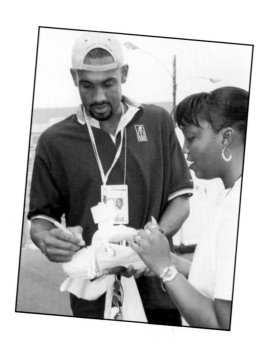

EVOLUTION

One day at basketball practice at Duke University, Grant Hill quietly told his teammate Antonio Lang, "I'm going to dunk the ball from the foul line." Grant had never tried the move before, but he was certain he could do it. He started at half court, dribbled the ball quickly as he picked up speed, and left the ground at the foul line. His body made a perfect arc toward the basket, and he stuffed the ball through the hoop just before returning to the ground. It was a move few players—pro or college—could do, but Grant didn't parade around the court afterwards, bragging about the accomplishment. "He just did it, and that was that," said Lang.

Performing with skill and grace, without letting his ego show, is what Grant Hill is all about. He inherited his athletic ability and his drive to succeed from his parents, Calvin and Janet Hill. They also instilled in him a sense of modesty and a respect for the feelings of others. Calvin was an All-America football player at Yale and a top running back in the National Football League for 11 years. His mother, who roomed in the same suite with Hillary Rodham Clinton at Wellesley College, has been a leading business consultant in Washington, D.C., for many years.

Though Grant is an only child, his parents didn't spoil him when he was growing up. Instead, they were quite strict. Some of Grant's friends even called his mother "The General." She gave out lots of orders that Grant had to obey exactly or be punished. One of the worst punishments was to keep him from playing sports.

Grant's parents, Calvin and Janet Hill, provided a strong support system for their son. Stressing determination, hard work, and team loyalty, they helped Grant develop the sports philosophy that he follows today.

Being the son of a professional athlete, Grant was always around sports and great players. In fact, it was a Hall of Fame quarterback who picked out his name. For the first few days after he was born on October 5, 1972, Grant was known as "Little Boy Hill" because his parents couldn't decide between several different names. Finally, Calvin's Dallas Cowboys teammate Roger Staubach announced, "It's time to name the child, and we're going to name him Grant."

Grant wasn't a "little boy" for very long. As an infant, his legs grew so quickly that he had to wear leg braces to bed to prevent his becoming bowlegged. The doctor even suggested breaking both his legs to help straighten them, but his parents refused to let that happen. Luckily, the braces did their job, and Grant's legs grew long and straight. He was nearly 6-foot-4 by the eighth grade and was a skilled and versatile athlete, first at soccer and later at basketball.

Grant grew up in a wealthy suburb of Virginia after his father was traded by the Cowboys to the Washington Redskins.

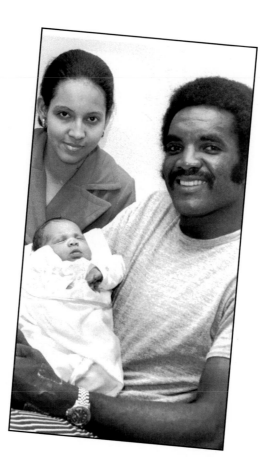

Grant was five days old and dubbed the "littlest Cowboy" in a newspaper photograph with his parents in 1972. His dad, Calvin, was a star running back for the Dallas Cowboys and later played for the Washington Redskins.

Football was the one team sport Grant's parents did not allow him to play. They didn't want him to risk getting injured. They also wanted to avoid any ego problems that might arise from being compared to his father.

Secretly, Calvin Hill hoped his son would decide to play football in high school and go on to be a gridiron star. But, by then, Grant had found his own sport in which to excel: basketball.

With his height and the grace and stamina he had developed playing soccer, Grant was a natural on the basketball court. But, out of modesty, he was reluctant to go out for his high school varsity team as a freshman. Most of his friends were playing junior varsity, and Grant didn't want to act like he was better than they were. Between them, the coach and Calvin convinced Grant to try out for

the varsity. He not only made the South Lakes High School starting team as a freshman, but even received his first college recruitment letter that year. It came from Denny Crum, the coach at highly ranked Louisville, who had received reports of the young man's talent and wanted to catch Grant's attention long before he was ready to choose a college.

During his high school career, Grant showed how multitalented a basketball player he was. He could handle the ball like a guard, shoot from the outside like a small forward, and rebound like a power forward. He was selected Northern Virginia Player of the Year three times and was named to *Parade Magazine*'s All-American team. But basketball wasn't his only interest. He was an honors student and a pretty good musician, too, able to play piano, drums, trombone, and bass guitar. "My parents wanted me to be cultured," he said, "so they had me doing everything. I can still play all of those instruments." He has even played the piano as a guest on the *Late Show With David Letterman* television program.

Exhibiting leadership skills and fierce determination on the court, Grant led Duke's Blue Devils to the NCAA finals three times.

By the time Grant became a high school basketball star, his father had retired from the NFL and had time to watch his son play. Calvin soon began a ritual that has continued throughout Grant's college and pro career. He watches each of Grant's games closely, in person or on television, not just as a fan but as if he were playing himself. Then after the game, he and Grant conduct a "PGA"—post-game analysis. They go over the game, play by play, and Calvin gives his opinion on what his son should have done or should be working on.

"My mother thought it was so funny," Grant recalls. "She'd say, 'Calvin, the boy scored 25 points.' But my dad was so intense. He'd say 'You've got to be prepared. You've got to focus.' Some people get their competitive fire through brothers or friends. I got it from my dad."

When it came time to choose a college for both education and basketball, the Hill family was fairly certain that the University of North Carolina was the right place. Then Grant made a side trip to Duke to

talk to coach Mike Krzyzewski. "Coach K" was one of the few coaches trying to recruit Grant who didn't promise him a starting position. Instead, he told the young player that he would have to earn his spot on the team and his playing time on the court. The challenge appealed to Grant, and he decided to go to Duke.

During the next four years, Grant helped the Blue Devils reach the Final Four three times and earn two national championships. Just as in high school, he proved he could do it all. He became the first player in the history of the prestigious Atlantic Coast Conference (ACC) to record more than 1,900 points, 700 rebounds, 400 assists, 200 steals, and 100 blocked shots. He was named to the first- or second-team All-America squad following his sophomore, junior, and senior seasons and was honored as the best defensive player in college basketball after his junior year.

Grant's talent was not the only quality that set him apart from other college players. His solid work ethic, humility, and commitment to team play also made him unique. He became the Blue Devils' leader in both attitude and action—even when he wasn't considered the team's "star."

During the 1991-92 season, for example, Duke's best-known player was center Christian Laettner. Most basketball fans remember that Laettner sank a miracle shot at the buzzer to beat Kentucky in overtime during the 1992 NCAA tournament, enabling Duke to reach the Final Four and earn its second straight championship. But not many people realize that it was Grant Hill who threw a perfect pass the length of the court to Laettner to set up the winning shot. The play didn't make Grant famous, but it did help Duke win. That's what mattered most to Grant.

Grant's years at Duke anchored his sense of team pride and cultivated his leadership abilities. His numerous successes are marked by a series of memorable events, like his perfect pass to Christian Laettner, center, that helped the Blue Devils win their second straight NCAA championship.

The next year, Grant suffered a foot injury that sidelined him the last two months of the season. Without him in the lineup, Duke was unable to win a third consecutive title. Before his senior year, however, he made an uncharacteristic boast. He guaranteed sportswriters that Duke would be champs again in 1994. The possibility seemed fairly remote. After all, Christian Laettner and All-America guard Bobby Hurley had graduated, and most of the team's current players were young and inexperienced, except for Grant and his roommate Antonio Lang.

Coach K told his senior star, "Don't be afraid to be great." Grant listened. He led the club in points, assists, and steals and was named a first-team All-American and ACC Player of the Year. With Grant leading the way, the Blue Devils unexpectedly powered their way through the preliminary rounds of the NCAA tournament to reach the finals against top-ranked Arkansas. Even though Arkansas beat Duke in the championship game, Grant and his teammates were proud of their accomplishment. "We

During his senior year at Duke, Grant Hill was named a first-team All-American and ACC Player of the Year. He then became a star player for the Detroit Pistons.

weren't the most talented team by far," Grant noted, "but we played with focus, toughness, and unbridled confidence." Just like their leader.

Two major events happened in Grant's life in June 1994. He graduated from Duke, and he was chosen by the Detroit Pistons as the third overall pick in the NBA draft. He was quickly swept up into a world of professional sports and high-level advertising. Grant's image as an unselfish superstar in college set him apart from some of the other top rookies and veterans in the league, who often let their egos dominate their talent.

"The league has taken a big hit in the last few years because of a few boorish stars," Grant noted. "I think they see me as a chance to start over. It's a hot and uncomfortable spotlight sometimes, but the upside has been tremendous." That upside included an eight-year contract for nearly $50 million, commercial endorsements for three major companies, and even his own line of athletic clothing and his own website on the Internet (www.grant-hill.com) sponsored by FILA. The company had chosen as its motto "Change the Game" and saw Grant as the perfect combination of outstanding player and positive role model that could fit that motto.

Grant saw the fame and money he was receiving as a way to bring about changes for other people as well. He made sure that FILA included in his contract an agreement to fund summer basketball camps for needy children. He also persuaded other companies to join him in

Basketball commissioner David Stern welcomes Grant Hill to the NBA. The Detroit Pistons chose Grant as the third overall pick in the NBA draft.

financing repairs for basketball courts in poor areas of Detroit. His first Thanksgiving in Detroit, Grant spent $10,000 of his own money to pay for dinners he personally helped deliver to senior citizens.

He got things done on the basketball court as well, quickly establishing himself as one of the top stars in the league. Grant scored 25 points and grabbed 10 rebounds in his first pro game against the Los Angeles Lakers on November 4, 1994, and maintained consistently high numbers throughout his rookie season. Fans around the country loved his combination of exciting talent and humble personality, and they made him the first rookie in the history of the NBA to lead the league in voting for the All-Star Game, topping even Michael Jordan and Shaquille O'Neal. At season's end, he also earned another honor—being named co-Rookie of the Year with Dallas Mavericks star Jason Kidd. He took his Rookie of the Year trophy home to Virginia to put next to the one his father had earned in the NFL in 1970.

Grant improved on the court in his second season, under the direction of new coach Doug Collins, and Detroit made the playoffs for the first time in four years. Showing his versatility, Grant led the club in minutes, scoring average, rebounds, blocks, and assists and also led the league in "triple-doubles"—games in which he achieved double-figure totals in points, rebounds, and assists.

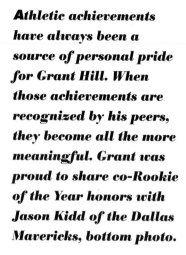

Athletic achievements have always been a source of personal pride for Grant Hill. When those achievements are recognized by his peers, they become all the more meaningful. Grant was proud to share co-Rookie of the Year honors with Jason Kidd of the Dallas Mavericks, bottom photo.

Grant's ranking as one of the top basketball players in the world was confirmed when he was named to Dream Team III, the United States' basketball squad for the 1996 Olympic Games in Atlanta. While at Duke, Grant had missed out on the 1992 Games and had felt a little cheated when the U.S. Olympic Committee sent mostly NBA players to represent the United States in Barcelona, Spain. This time he was a key component in the

U.S. gold-medal winning effort. In a game against China, Grant scored 19 points and had five assists, four rebounds, and five steals—a typical all-around performance. "Playing in the Olympics was a great honor and a dream come true," he said.

Since Grant Hill arrived in Detroit, the Pistons are definitely on an upswing. The team's future seems brighter than it has in many years, largely because of Grant's play and the image he projects to teammates both on and off the court.

"When I came to Detroit," said Coach Collins, "I knew we had a winner in Grant Hill. Grant is all about winning."

Representing his country as part of Dream Team III was a crowning moment in a long list of achievements for Grant Hill.

VOICES

ON HIS CHILDHOOD
AND FAMILY:

"My father was laid back, but
my mom was definitely strict.
My friends used to call her 'The
General.' She could be tough, and
she didn't care who you were.
One time my mom got mad
at one of my friends and
punished him by send-
ing him to *my* room."

Grant Hill

"We didn't think we were that strict. We would always strive for excellence, not settle for mediocrity. We would lead by example."

Janet Hill, Grant's mother

"With my mother, no matter what I do (on the court), it's great. I could have a terrible game, and she'll say, 'Grant, you played great.' But my father is never satisfied. But that's cool because I'm never satisfied either. And that's what drives me."

Grant Hill

Grant Hill's mother, Janet, instilled in him a sense of modesty and a respect for the feelings of others.

ON HIS PLAYING STYLE:

"Even when I started playing basketball and got some recognition as
a freshman in high school, I had a
problem with being known as 'Son
of ex-NFL star Calvin Hill.' I just
had a tough time with that. I didn't
want to be identified as the son
of anyone. I wanted to be
identified as Grant Hill."

Grant Hill

"There are only two things that matter. You've got to have fun playing ball. And you can't have fun unless you win."

Grant Hill

"Grant Hill is the best player I've ever coached, period. But he's a reluctant superstar. He wants to be the best, but he doesn't want to separate himself from the team."

Mike Krzyzewski,
Duke coach

"His focus is to win. He doesn't go out and try to score 40 points a night. He just tries to help us win games, and that's what makes him special."

Joe Dumars,
Detroit Pistons teammate

"The game will become easier for him as our team gets better. Right now, he has to work too hard to help us. But he wants to be great, and he's headed in that direction. When he reaches his peak, he'll be in the mold of Julius Erving—scoring, rebounding, and assisting."

Doug Collins,
Detroit Pistons coach

"He's been a great player since day one. I don't know whether we've had a better player in a long time other than Michael Jordan who can take you off the dribble and get to the basket. He's also got explosiveness, and he's developing every aspect of his game, particularly his outside shot. He's going to get better and better."

Chuck Daly, basketball
analyst and former Pistons coach

Joe Dumars, top photo, Doug Collins, center, and Chuck Daly have high praise for Grant Hill.

"I think every player growing up
wants to be in this situation—making a lot of money and being looked
on as a savior of a franchise. Nah, I
don't think everybody wants to be
in this position, but I do. Hopefully,
I can do a good job."

Grant Hill

"Now that I have children, I particularly appreciate Grant Hill. If I could say I want my children to be like anyone, that person is Grant Hill."

Joe Dumars

"We're tired of the trash-talking, in-your-face, slam-dunk, rip-the-rim-down scenario. What Grant brings is total class, elegance, grace, and the ability to communicate effectively with all people."

Jap Trimble, FILA executive

Dedication to the game, outstanding skill, respect for his teammates, and appreciation for his fans are just some of the elements that contribute to Grant Hill's popularity.

"He's just as good a guy as he is a basketball player. He believes he's a regular person who's gifted to play basketball."

Antonio Lang, Duke teammate

"I enjoy beating a guy to the ball, or dunking on him. And I'm excited when I do. But when I dunk, I don't point my finger or get in someone's face. I guess that makes me different from a lot of guys in the NBA, but I've never derived pleasure from making someone else feel bad or angry. That probably goes back to my wanting to be everybody's friend (when I was a kid). When the game's over, I don't want the guys on the other team to hate me."

Grant Hill

Since Grant Hill arrived in Detroit, the Pistons have been on an upswing.

OVATIONS